This journal belongs to

_____

Date begun

_____

Date ended

_____

The Prayer of Jesus
Prayer Journal

secrets to real intimacy with God

Based on *The Prayer of Jesus*
by Hank Hanegraaff

W PUBLISHING GROUP™

www.wpublishinggroup.com

A Division of Thomas Nelson, Inc.
www.ThomasNelson.com

The Prayer of Jesus Prayer Journal

Copyright © 2001 by Hank Hanegraaff

Published by The W Publishing Group, a division of Thomas Nelson Publishers, P.O. Box 141000, Nashville, TN 37214. All rights reserved. No portion of this publication may be reproduced, stored in a retrieval system or transmitted in any form or by any means—electronic, mechanical, photocopying, recording, or any other—except for brief quotations in printed reviews, without the prior written permission of the publisher.

Unless otherwise indicated, all Scripture quotations in this book are taken from the Holy Bible, New International Version (NIV). Copyright © 1973, 1978, 1984 by International Bible Society. Used by permission of Zondervan Bible Publishers. All rights reserved.

Produced with the assistance of The Livingstone Corporation. Project staff includes Paige Drygas, Katie Gieser, and Neil Wilson.

Interior design by Mark Wainwright

ISBN 0-8499-1750-6

Printed in the United States of America

01 02 03 04 05 06 07 BVG 7 6 5 4 3 2 1

Dedication

To my daughter Christina, who loves to pray. Christ is not only foremost in her name but in her life.

Introduction

Dear Partner in Prayer,

The fact that you now hold *The Prayer of Jesus* PRAYER JOURNAL in your hands is a direct answer to my prayers. It means that you have joined an ever-growing number of Christians who are serious about taking their prayer lives to the next level. Rather than merely looking for techniques through which you can get God to answer your prayers, you have graduated to seeing prayer as an opportunity for developing intimacy with the very One who knit you together in your mother's womb.

The reality is that most of us merely snorkel in the surface waters of prayer and succeed only in burning our backs. Deep is where we step out of the shallow tide pool of our hearts into the boundless ocean of God's power and presence. It is where we get beyond surface things and plunge into a deep relationship with our Creator. Jesus wanted his disciples to venture out of the shallow waters of prayer. Thus, when they began begging him to teach them how to pray, he offered the pattern of his own personal prayer life as a brilliant shaft leading deep into the ocean of prayer. The prayer of Jesus is the entryway into an ever-deepening experience with God.

Here's how I suggest you use your personal prayer journal.

First, if you have not done so already, discover your secret place. We all desperately need a place away from the invasive sounds of this world so that we can hear the sounds of another place. God has sent us sixty-six love letters etched in heavenly handwriting. And the more you meditate upon those words in your secret place, the clearer his voice will be.

Second, remember that prayer begins with a humble *faith* in the love and resources of your heavenly Father. Such faith inevitably leads to *adoration* as you express your love and longing for an ever-deepening relationship with God. The more you get to know him in the fullness of his majesty, the more you will be inclined to *confess* your sins and *thank* him for his goodness in supplying all your needs.

Third, The *Prayer of Jesus* PRAYER JOURNAL is designed to aid you in making the prayer that Jesus taught his disciples to pray the pattern for the rest of your prayer life. As you work through the journal you will grow in understanding that the prayer of Jesus is not a prayer mantra but a prayer manner that will guide you into an ever-richer and more rewarding relationship with your Lord.

The prayer of Jesus has absolutely revolutionized my prayer life. And it is my fervent prayer that it will revolutionize your prayer life as well!

With warmest regards,

Hank Hanegraaff

Our Father in heaven,
hallowed be your name,
your kingdom come,
your will be done
on earth as it is in heaven.
Give us today our daily bread.
Forgive us our debts,
as we also have forgiven our debtors.
And lead us not into temptation,
but deliver us from the evil one,
for yours is the kingdom
and the power and the glory forever.
Amen.

Matthew 6:9–13

chapter one

Lord, Teach Us *Now* to Pray

The disciples circle around the Master teacher, urgency sketched on their faces. One of them, perhaps Peter, blurts out... "Lord, teach us *now* to pray!"

Question: As you begin the process of prayer journaling, does the Master teacher have your undivided attention?

TEACH ME YOUR WAY, O LORD, AND I WILL WALK IN YOUR TRUTH; GIVE ME AN UNDIVIDED HEART, THAT I MAY FEAR YOUR NAME. PSALM 86:11

Reflections

Pray

Lord, teach me to withdraw from the distractions
of my life and to make prayer a priority . . .

The disciples may have been uncertain of what made Christ's face seem as though it glowed, but of one thing they were certain: Whatever it was, they wanted it, and they wanted it *now!*

Question: On a scale of one to ten, how high is prayer on your list of daily priorities?

ONE DAY JESUS WAS PRAYING IN A CERTAIN PLACE. WHEN HE FINISHED, ONE OF HIS DISCIPLES SAID TO HIM, "LORD, TEACH US TO PRAY, JUST AS JOHN TAUGHT HIS DISCIPLES." LUKE 11:1

Reflections

_____

_____

_____

_____

_____

_____

_____

_____

_____

_____

_____

_____

_____

_____

_____

_____

_____

_____

_____

Pray

Lord, teach me to pray. I humbly come to you,
my Teacher, to learn from your example . . .

Jesus could have pointed his disciples to the prayers of Joshua, Jepthah, or, yes, Jabez. But he didn't. Jesus knew that his disciples would never properly understand *examples* of prayer without first understanding *principles* of prayer.

Question: Why must biblical examples of prayer always be understood in light of principles of prayer?

THIS, THEN IS HOW YOU SHOULD PRAY ... MATTHEW 6:9A

Reflections

_____

_____

_____

_____

_____

_____

_____

_____

_____

_____

_____

_____

_____

_____

_____

_____

_____

_____

_____

_____

Pray

Teacher, please rid my heart of any
misconceptions I have about prayer . . .

Jesus did not give us a prayer mantra; he gave us a prayer pattern.

Question: A *mantra* is a mystical formula, meant as a form of prayer. How does a "prayer mantra" differ from a "prayer pattern"?

THE PRAYER OF A RIGHTEOUS MAN IS POWERFUL AND EFFECTIVE. JAMES 5:16B

Reflections

_____

_____

_____

_____

_____

_____

_____

_____

_____

_____

_____

_____

_____

_____

_____

_____

_____

_____

Pray

Jesus, teach me to follow the pattern that
you gave to your disciples . . .

Was Peter speaking for you when he pleaded, "Lord, teach us *now* to pray?"

Question: What are your motivations for studying prayer?

_____

_____

_____

_____

_____

_____

_____

_____

_____

_____

_____

_____

ONE OF THOSE DAYS JESUS WENT OUT TO A MOUNTAINSIDE TO PRAY, AND SPENT THE NIGHT PRAYING TO GOD. LUKE 6:12

Reflections

_____

_____

_____

_____

_____

_____

_____

_____

_____

_____

_____

_____

_____

_____

_____

_____

_____

_____

_____

Pray

Lord, give me an undivided heart . . .

chapter two

The Secret

The secret to prayer is secret prayer.

Question: The very first principle Jesus teaches his disciples regarding prayer is that our goal should never be the approval of men, but rather the approval of our Father in heaven. What happens when these priorities are reversed?

_____

_____

_____

_____

_____

_____

_____

_____

_____

_____

BUT WHEN YOU PRAY, GO INTO YOUR ROOM, CLOSE THE DOOR AND PRAY TO YOUR FATHER, WHO IS UNSEEN. THEN YOUR FATHER, WHO SEES WHAT IS DONE IN SECRET, WILL REWARD YOU. MATTHEW 6:6

Reflections

_____

_____

_____

_____

_____

_____

_____

_____

_____

_____

_____

_____

_____

_____

_____

_____

_____

_____

_____

Pray

Father, help my quiet moments with you to be the
defining moments of my life . . .

*P*rayer is not a magic formula to get things from God. Communing with God in prayer is itself the prize.

Question: Do you treasure fellowship with the Father? How does your answer to that question affect your prayers?

_____

_____

_____

_____

_____

_____

_____

_____

_____

_____

_____

_____

_____

JESUS OFTEN WITHDREW TO LONELY PLACES AND PRAYED. LUKE 5:16

Reflections

_____

_____

_____

_____

_____

_____

_____

_____

_____

_____

_____

_____

_____

_____

_____

_____

_____

_____

_____

Pray

Father, help me to experience ever more fully the blessing of resting
in your presence through the finished work of Jesus Christ...

*I*n our fast food culture we are forever looking for instant gratification. A cacophony of voices promises us quick fixes and instant cures when in reality there are none.

Question: How can you change your mindset so that communion with God itself becomes your goal in prayer?

LET US DRAW NEAR TO GOD WITH A SINCERE HEART IN FULL ASSURANCE OF FAITH.... HEBREWS 10:22

Reflections

_____

_____

_____

_____

_____

_____

_____

_____

_____

_____

_____

_____

_____

_____

_____

_____

_____

_____

Pray

Lord, stir in me a greater desire to commune with you . . .

The tragedy of contemporary Christianity is that we measure the success of our prayer life by the size and scope of our accomplishments, rather than the strength of our relationships with God. All too often we are fixated on our outwardness, while God is focused on our inwardness.

Question: There is a God-shaped vacuum in our lives that only God can fill. What happens when we attempt to fill that vacuum with outward successes rather than silent adoration and steady devotion?

THE LORD DOES NOT LOOK AT THE THINGS MAN LOOKS AT. MAN LOOKS AT THE OUTWARD APPEARANCE, BUT THE LORD LOOKS AT THE HEART.

1 SAMUEL 16:7B

Reflections

_____

_____

_____

_____

_____

_____

_____

_____

_____

_____

_____

_____

_____

_____

_____

_____

_____

_____

Pray

Lord, help me to practice silent adoration and steady devotion
rather than focusing on mere outward appearances . . .

As human beings we want instant formulas, but God wants intimate fellowship.

Question: In your own words, what is the secret to prayer?

_____

_____

_____

_____

_____

_____

_____

_____

_____

_____

_____

_____

_____

COME NEAR TO GOD AND HE WILL COME NEAR TO YOU. JAMES 4:8A

Reflections

Pray

Lord, help me to yearn for intimate fellowship with you . . .

Rather than fixate on earthly vanities, such as the admiration of men, we ought to focus on such eternal verities as the approval of the Master.

Question: What is the reward for a life of faithful prayer?

BUT STORE UP FOR YOURSELVES TREASURES IN HEAVEN, WHERE MOTH AND RUST DO NOT DESTROY, AND WHERE THIEVES DO NOT BREAK IN AND STEAL.

MATTHEW 6:20

Reflections

_____

_____

_____

_____

_____

_____

_____

_____

_____

_____

_____

_____

_____

_____

_____

_____

_____

_____

Pray

Father, thank you for forgiving all my sins and declaring
me righteous by your grace through faith alone in Jesus Christ.
Now I want my treasure to be in heaven with you . . .

Your Father Knows

Your Father Knows

All of us have been tempted to look for shortcuts to success. And nowhere is this truer than when it comes to our prayer lives.

Question: The second principle of prayer that Jesus teaches his disciples is that our heavenly Father already knows what we need before we ask him. Thus, he gives us gifts we fail to ask for and withholds some gifts we do ask for—for he knows that if he gives us some of those things they would only serve to ruin us. Think back through your own prayers. Can you see how much better God's gifts are than the ones you so often ask for?

_____

_____

_____

_____

_____

_____

_____

_____

_____

BUT SMALL IS THE GATE AND NARROW THE ROAD THAT LEADS TO LIFE, AND ONLY A FEW FIND IT. MATTHEW 7:14

Reflections

Pray

Lord, let me not be distracted by any hollow,
easy shortcuts to prayer . . .

Before Jesus launches into the principles of prayer through the most beautiful, symmetrical, and majestic of all biblical prayers, he first warns his disciples against praying as pagans do. The last thing he wants us to do is turn the prayer of Jesus into what the Scriptures refer to as "vain repetitions."

Question: How does Jesus describe the prayers of pagans?

_____

_____

_____

_____

_____

_____

_____

_____

_____

AND WHEN YOU PRAY, DO NOT KEEP ON BABBLING LIKE PAGANS, FOR THEY THINK THEY WILL BE HEARD BECAUSE OF THEIR MANY WORDS. DO NOT BE LIKE THEM, FOR YOUR FATHER KNOWS WHAT YOU NEED BEFORE YOU ASK HIM.

MATTHEW 6:7–8

Reflections

_____

_____

_____

_____

_____

_____

_____

_____

_____

_____

_____

_____

_____

_____

_____

_____

_____

_____

_____

Pray

Father, keep me from vain repetitions and doubt . . .

Relationships are cemented not just by giving and getting but by love and communication.

⁓

Question: Is your relationship with God based more on giving and getting than on love and communication?

_____

_____

_____

_____

_____

_____

_____

_____

_____

_____

_____

_____

_____

LOVE THE LORD YOUR GOD WITH ALL YOUR HEART AND WITH ALL YOUR SOUL AND WITH ALL YOUR MIND AND WITH ALL YOUR STRENGTH. MARK 12:30

Reflections

_____

_____

_____

_____

_____

_____

_____

_____

_____

_____

_____

_____

_____

_____

_____

_____

_____

_____

Pray

Lord, I want to invest in an intimate,
personal relationship with you . . .

*P*rayer begins with a humble faith in the love and resources of our heavenly Father. Thus, prayer becomes a means through which we learn to lean more heavily upon him and less heavily upon ourselves.

Question: Faith is a channel of living trust between you and your Lord. It is only as good as the object in which it is placed. Is your faith in your faith? Or is your faith in your Lord?

IF YOU REMAIN IN ME AND MY WORDS REMAIN IN YOU, ASK WHATEVER YOU WISH, AND IT WILL BE GIVEN YOU. JOHN 15:7

Reflections

_____

_____

_____

_____

_____

_____

_____

_____

_____

_____

_____

_____

_____

_____

_____

_____

_____

_____

_____

_____

_____

Pray

Father, help me to build my faith by knowing
you more through your Word . . .

Prayer without adoration is like a body without a soul.... it is not only incomplete, but it just doesn't work. Through adoration we express our genuine, heartfelt love and longing for God.

Question: Why is adoration the soul of prayer?

_____

_____

_____

_____

_____

Write a simple prayer of adoration, praising God for who he is.

_____

_____

_____

_____

_____

COME, LET US BOW DOWN IN WORSHIP,
  LET US KNEEL BEFORE THE LORD OUR MAKER. PSALM 95:6

Reflections

_____
_____
_____
_____
_____
_____
_____
_____
_____
_____
_____
_____
_____
_____
_____
_____
_____
_____
_____
_____

Pray

Father, I adore you . . .

The more we get to know God in the fullness of his majesty, the more we are inclined to confess our sins. While unconfessed sin will not break our union with God, it will break our communion with God.

Question: What effect does unconfessed sin have on your relationship with God?

_____

_____

_____

_____

_____

Write a simple prayer of confession, specifically admitting to God how you have sinned.

_____

_____

_____

_____

_____

IF WE CONFESS OUR SINS, HE IS FAITHFUL AND JUST AND WILL FORGIVE US OUR SINS AND PURIFY US FROM ALL UNRIGHTEOUSNESS. 1 JOHN 1:9

Reflections

_____

_____

_____

_____

_____

_____

_____

_____

_____

_____

_____

_____

_____

_____

_____

_____

_____

_____

_____

Pray

Lord, I come to you in repentance . . .

*S*cripture teaches us to "enter his gates with thanksgiving and his courts with praise." Failure to do so is the stuff of pagan babblings and carnal Christianity.

Question: How does thanksgiving help us to overcome our tendency to forget what God has done for us?

Write down some of the things for which you are thankful that immediately come to mind.

ENTER HIS GATES WITH THANKSGIVING AND HIS COURTS WITH PRAISE; GIVE THANKS TO HIM AND PRAISE HIS NAME. PSALM 100:4

Reflections

_____

_____

_____

_____

_____

_____

_____

_____

_____

_____

_____

_____

_____

_____

_____

_____

_____

_____

_____

Pray

Lord Jesus, thank you for all the blessings you have given me . . .

The purpose of supplication is not to pressure God into providing us with provisions and pleasures, but rather to conform us to his purposes.

Question: If we view supplication as the sole sum and substance of prayer, we have missed the main point. Have you missed the main point?

THIS IS THE CONFIDENCE WE HAVE IN APPROACHING GOD: THAT IF WE ASK ANYTHING ACCORDING TO HIS WILL, HE HEARS US. AND IF WE KNOW THAT HE HEARS US—WHATEVER WE ASK—WE KNOW THAT WE HAVE WHAT WE ASKED OF HIM. 1 JOHN 5:14–15

Reflections

_____

_____

_____

_____

_____

_____

_____

_____

_____

_____

_____

_____

_____

_____

_____

_____

_____

_____

_____

_____

Pray

Lord, may my prayer life be characterized by faith, adoration,
confession, and thanksgiving, as well as supplication . . .

Your Father Knows

While our Father knows what we need before we even ask, our supplications are in and of themselves an acknowledgement of our dependence on him. And that alone is reason enough to pray without ceasing.

Question: How do our prayers reveal our dependence on God?

PRAY CONTINUALLY. 1 THESSALONIANS 5:17

Reflections

_____

_____

_____

_____

_____

_____

_____

_____

_____

_____

_____

_____

_____

_____

_____

_____

_____

_____

Pray

Lord, I depend fully on your strength, not on my own . . .

Building Our Relationship

Jesus made every word he spoke count. The words of the prayer he taught us to pray are treasures of incalculable value lying deep beneath the cobalt waters of a vast ocean. Like the siren call of the mermaids, his words beckon those snorkeling with burnt backs in shallow tide pools to don scuba gear and descend into the prayer's glorious depths. There await unfathomed resources and riches that can scarcely be described to those living on the surface.

Question: Why is the prayer Jesus taught his disciples to pray infinitely more valuable than any other prayer pattern?

HE TAUGHT AS ONE WHO HAD AUTHORITY, AND NOT AS THEIR TEACHERS OF THE LAW. MATTHEW 7:29

Reflections

_____

_____

_____

_____

_____

_____

_____

_____

_____

_____

_____

_____

_____

_____

_____

_____

_____

_____

_____

Pray

Lord, help me to discover the treasures you have placed
within the words you taught your disciples to pray . . .

To the disciples, the first words of the prayer of Jesus must have been nothing short of scandalous. They were not even permitted to say the name of God aloud, let alone refer to him as "our Father." Yet, that is precisely how Jesus taught his disciples to pray.

Question: What gives us the privilege of referring to God as "our Father"?

_____

_____

_____

_____

_____

_____

_____

_____

_____

_____

_____

_____

YET TO ALL WHO RECEIVED HIM, TO THOSE WHO BELIEVED IN HIS NAME, HE GAVE THE RIGHT TO BECOME CHILDREN OF GOD. JOHN 1:12

Reflections

_____

_____

_____

_____

_____

_____

_____

_____

_____

_____

_____

_____

_____

_____

_____

_____

_____

Pray

God, thank you that we are no longer illegitimate children but
rather sons and daughters by adoption through faith alone in
the very One who taught us to pray, "Our Father . . ."

*J*esus taught his disciples to qualify the phrase "our Father" with the words "in heaven." In doing so he is teaching us that God transcends time and space. We can address him with intimacy but never impudence. He is the sovereign Creator; we are but sinful creatures.

Question: How does our culture contribute to a diminished view of God and an exalted view of man?

_____

_____

_____

_____

_____

_____

_____

_____

[GOD'S] DOMINION IS AN ETERNAL DOMINION; HIS KINGDOM ENDURES FROM GENERATION TO GENERATION. ALL THE PEOPLES OF THE EARTH ARE REGARDED AS NOTHING. HE DOES AS HE PLEASES WITH THE POWERS OF HEAVEN AND THE PEOPLES OF THE EARTH. NO ONE CAN HOLD BACK HIS HAND OR SAY TO HIM: "WHAT HAVE YOU DONE?" DANIEL 4:34C–35

Reflections

Pray

Lord, teach me to magnify your majesty and yet come into your
presence with the words "Abba, Father ..."

The initial petition of the prayer of Jesus is that God's name be made holy. To pray "hallowed be your name" is to put the emphasis on God first, exactly where it belongs.

Question: To pray "hallowed be your name" is to pray that
- God be given the reverence his holiness demands;
- God's church be led by faithful pastors and preserved from pitfalls;
- we be kept from language that profanes God's name;
- our thought lives remain holy.

Can you think of other ways to personalize this petition?

HOLY, HOLY, HOLY IS THE LORD ALMIGHTY;
  THE WHOLE EARTH IS FULL OF HIS GLORY. ISAIAH 6:3B

Reflections

_____

_____

_____

_____

_____

_____

_____

_____

_____

_____

_____

_____

_____

_____

_____

_____

_____

_____

Pray

Lord, help me to realize anew today that my moniker
and meager attempts at ministry are meaningless
unless your name is magnified . . .

chapter five

The City of God

*I*n teaching us to pray "your kingdom come," Jesus was first and foremost teaching us to petition our heavenly Father to expand his rule over the territory of our hearts. It is an invitation to embrace the kingdom of Christ in every aspect of our lives.

Question: Does Christ reign in every area of your life? What parts do you tend to hold back from him?

Do not conform any longer to the pattern of this world, but be transformed by the renewing of your mind. Then you will be able to test and approve what God's will is—his good, pleasing and perfect will. Romans 12:2

Reflections

_____

_____

_____

_____

_____

_____

_____

_____

_____

_____

_____

_____

_____

_____

_____

_____

_____

_____

_____

Pray

Dear Lord, expand your rule over the territory of my heart . . .

To pray "your kingdom come" is to pray that God would use our witness for the expansion of his kingdom.

Question: Are there people within the sphere of your influence to whom the Holy Spirit is prompting you to testify through your life, your love, or your lips? If so, list one or more of those people below and begin to include them in your daily petitions.

THE HARVEST IS PLENTIFUL, BUT THE WORKERS ARE FEW. ASK THE LORD OF THE HARVEST, THEREFORE, TO SEND OUT WORKERS INTO HIS HARVEST FIELD.

LUKE 10:2

Reflections

_____

_____

_____

_____

_____

_____

_____

_____

_____

_____

_____

_____

_____

_____

_____

_____

_____

_____

_____

Pray

Lord, use me to share your love with those I meet . . .

To pray "your kingdom come" is to recognize that Christ has already won the war, but the reality of his reign is not yet fully realized. At present we are sandwiched between the triumph of the cross and the termination of time.

Question: Often, in the midst of our day-to-day battles, we forget that the war has already been won. How can that truth change our whole outlook on life?

NOW THE DWELLING OF GOD IS WITH MEN, AND HE WILL LIVE WITH THEM. THEY WILL BE HIS PEOPLE, AND GOD HIMSELF WILL BE WITH THEM AND BE THEIR GOD. HE WILL WIPE EVERY TEAR FROM THEIR EYES. THERE WILL BE NO MORE DEATH OR MOURNING OR CRYING OR PAIN, FOR THE OLD ORDER OF THINGS HAS PASSED AWAY. REVELATION 21:3B–4

Reflections

_____

_____

_____

_____

_____

_____

_____

_____

_____

_____

_____

_____

_____

_____

_____

_____

_____

_____

_____

_____

_____

Pray

Jesus, your victory brings life. Come, Lord Jesus . . .

To pray "your will be done" is, first and foremost, recognition of the sovereignty of God. . . . We would be in deep trouble if God gave us everything for which we asked. The truth is we don't know what's best for us.

Question: Think of a past prayer request that, looking back, you know would not have been best for you. How would your life be different if God had answered your request the way you wanted?

IN THE SAME WAY, THE SPIRIT HELPS US IN OUR WEAKNESS. WE DO NOT KNOW WHAT WE OUGHT TO PRAY FOR, BUT THE SPIRIT HIMSELF INTERCEDES FOR US WITH GROANS THAT WORDS CANNOT EXPRESS. ROMANS 8:26

Reflections

Pray

Father, thank you that you give me what is best for me, not
always what I ask for . . .

To pray "your will be done" is daily recognition that our wills must be submitted to his will. In the yielded life there is great peace in knowing that God has every detail of our lives under control.

Question: Did you know that with the word "amen" you are in effect saying, "May it be so in accordance with the will of God"? Are you willing to bring every aspect of your life into conformity to the will of God?

_____

_____

_____

_____

_____

_____

_____

_____

_____

_____

_____

_____

AND WE KNOW THAT IN ALL THINGS GOD WORKS FOR THE GOOD OF THOSE WHO LOVE HIM, WHO HAVE BEEN CALLED ACCORDING TO HIS PURPOSE.

ROMANS 8:28

Reflections

_____

_____

_____

_____

_____

_____

_____

_____

_____

_____

_____

_____

_____

_____

_____

_____

_____

_____

_____

Pray

Lord, thank you for using even the difficult circumstances
in my life for my good and for your glory . . .

To pray "your will be done" is daily recognition that God will not spare us from trial and tribulation but rather use the fiery furnace to purge impurities from our lives.

Question: Why does the fact that God does not spare us from trials show that he loves us deeply?

BLESSED IS THE MAN WHO PERSEVERES UNDER TRIAL, BECAUSE WHEN HE HAS STOOD THE TEST, HE WILL RECEIVE THE CROWN OF LIFE THAT GOD HAS PROMISED TO THOSE WHO LOVE HIM. JAMES 1:12

Reflections

_____

_____

_____

_____

_____

_____

_____

_____

_____

_____

_____

_____

_____

_____

_____

_____

_____

_____

_____

_____

Pray

Lord, thank you that you don't always spare me from pain . . .

The prayer of Jesus is neatly divided into two parts. The first is focused on God's glory. The second is focused on our needs. From this point on we pray for ourselves—it is the third petition that brings the prayer of Jesus down to earth. Thus we pray "on earth as it is in heaven."

Question: What would the world be like if all those who claim to be followers of Christ worked to extend God's will on earth rather than their own?

I SAW THE HOLY CITY, THE NEW JERUSALEM, COMING DOWN OUT OF HEAVEN FROM GOD, PREPARED AS A BRIDE BEAUTIFULLY DRESSED FOR HER HUSBAND. REVELATION 21:2

Reflections

Pray

Dear Lord, may your name, your kingdom,
and your will be done on earth as it is in heaven . . .

chapter six

Bringing Our Requests

*P*etitioning our heavenly Father to *"give us today our daily bread"* encompasses all things that are necessary to sustain our bodies and lives.

Question: The word "bread" in the context of the prayer of Jesus can be rightly understood in a larger sense to encompass all things necessary for the peaceable and honest ordering of our lives. Which of these necessities do you find yourself taking for granted?

GIVE ME NEITHER POVERTY NOR RICHES, BUT GIVE ME ONLY MY DAILY BREAD. OTHERWISE, I MAY HAVE TOO MUCH AND DISOWN YOU AND SAY, "WHO IS THE LORD?" OR I MAY BECOME POOR AND STEAL, AND SO DISHONOR THE NAME OF MY GOD. PROVERBS 30:8–9

Reflections

_____

_____

_____

_____

_____

_____

_____

_____

_____

_____

_____

_____

_____

_____

_____

_____

_____

Pray

My heavenly Father, I thank you that every breath
is a gift to me from your loving hand . . .

When we ask our heavenly Father to *"give us today our daily bread,"* we pray in the plural. We do not pray as mere rugged individualists but as members of a community of faith.

Question: It is hard to pray "give" without being givers ourselves. Can you think of someone who needs your help today? Why not pray for that person right now—then take the next step and put feet to your faith!

I TELL YOU THE TRUTH, ANYONE WHO GIVES YOU A CUP OF WATER IN MY NAME BECAUSE YOU BELONG TO CHRIST WILL CERTAINLY NOT LOSE HIS REWARD. MARK 9:41

Reflections

_____

_____

_____

_____

_____

_____

_____

_____

_____

_____

_____

_____

_____

_____

_____

_____

_____

Pray

Dear Father, open my eyes to the needs of my brothers
and sisters around the world who suffer daily from
maladies ranging from droughts to deadly diseases . . .

When Jesus taught his disciples to pray *"give us today our daily bread"* he was reminding them that he would be there to sustain them spiritually as well as physically. Each time we partake of communion we are reminded that he is *"the bread of life."*

Question: What does it mean to say that "bread" symbolizes an aftertaste of salvation and a foretaste of the kingdom to come?

THEN JESUS DECLARED, "I AM THE BREAD OF LIFE. HE WHO COMES TO ME WILL NEVER GO HUNGRY, AND HE WHO BELIEVES IN ME WILL NEVER BE THIRSTY." JOHN 6:35

Reflections

_____

_____

_____

_____

_____

_____

_____

_____

_____

_____

_____

_____

_____

_____

_____

_____

_____

_____

Pray

Dear Jesus, I thank you that your body was broken and
your blood poured out to pay my debt in full . . .

chapter seven

The Compassion Award

One of the most riveting parables Jesus ever communicated to his disciples is found in Matthew 18:23–35. It was the story of two debtors and a Master who truly deserved a "Compassion Award." The point of the parable is that the debts we owe one another are like mere twenty dollar bills compared to the infinite debt we owe our heavenly Father.

Question: Are you truly mindful of the fact that you have been forgiven an infinite debt, and that it is a horrendous evil to even consider withholding forgiveness from those who seek it? If not, ask the Lord to help you be willing to forgive anyone who sincerely seeks your forgiveness.

AND WHEN YOU STAND PRAYING, IF YOU HOLD ANYTHING AGAINST ANYONE, FORGIVE HIM, SO THAT YOUR FATHER IN HEAVEN MAY FORGIVE YOU YOUR SINS. MARK 11:25

Reflections

Pray

Lord, let me keep others' sins against me in perspective
with my sins against you . . .

When we pray, "Forgive us our debts, as we also have forgiven our debtors," we are reminded of the infinite price that was paid so that we might be forgiven. We must be ever mindful that it was God himself who hung on the cross so that we could be reconciled to him for time and for eternity.

Question: Have you grown indifferent to Jesus' sacrifice, or is its meaning fresh for you each day? How can you rekindle your first love?

_____

_____

_____

_____

_____

_____

_____

_____

_____

_____

BUT HE WAS PIERCED FOR OUR TRANSGRESSIONS, HE WAS CRUSHED FOR OUR INIQUITIES; THE PUNISHMENT THAT BROUGHT US PEACE WAS UPON HIM, AND BY HIS WOUNDS WE ARE HEALED. ISAIAH 53:5

Reflections

Pray

Lord, thank you for the ultimate sacrifice of love
that you gave for me on the cross . . .

Brokenness is the road map by which we find our way back to an intimate relationship with God and compassion for one another.

Question: To what degree is your life marked by brokenness?

THE SACRIFICES OF GOD ARE A BROKEN SPIRIT; A BROKEN AND CONTRITE HEART, O GOD, YOU WILL NOT DESPISE. PSALM 51:17

Reflections

_____

_____

_____

_____

_____

_____

_____

_____

_____

_____

_____

_____

_____

_____

_____

_____

_____

_____

Pray

As Psalm 51:1 says, "Have mercy on me, O God,
according to your unfailing love; according to your
great compassion blot out my transgressions . . ."

If only we could learn to forgive and seek to be forgiven as quickly as children . . .

Question: Why does Christ encourage us to have childlike hearts and faith?

AND HE SAID: "I TELL YOU THE TRUTH, UNLESS YOU CHANGE AND BECOME LIKE LITTLE CHILDREN, YOU WILL NEVER ENTER THE KINGDOM OF HEAVEN."

MATTHEW 18:3

Reflections

_____

_____

_____

_____

_____

_____

_____

_____

_____

_____

_____

_____

_____

_____

_____

_____

_____

_____

_____

_____

_____

Pray

Father, I ask you to give me not a *childish* faith
but a *childlike* faith . . .

The Armor

The Armor

When you pray, "Lead us not into temptation, but deliver us from the evil one," you should immediately remember to put on the full armor of God so that you can take your stand against the devil's schemes.

Question: Are you intimately acquainted with each piece of the armor described in Ephesians 6:11–18? If not, are you willing to discover the power and protection locked up in each piece?

_____

_____

_____

_____

_____

_____

STAND FIRM THEN, WITH THE BELT OF TRUTH BUCKLED AROUND YOUR WAIST, WITH THE BREASTPLATE OF RIGHTEOUSNESS IN PLACE, AND WITH YOUR FEET FITTED WITH THE READINESS THAT COMES FROM THE GOSPEL OF PEACE. IN ADDITION TO ALL THIS, TAKE UP THE SHIELD OF FAITH, WITH WHICH YOU CAN EXTINGUISH ALL OF THE FLAMING ARROWS OF THE EVIL ONE. TAKE THE HELMET OF SALVATION AND THE SWORD OF THE SPIRIT, WHICH IS THE WORD OF GOD. AND PRAY IN THE SPIRIT ON ALL OCCASIONS WITH ALL KINDS OF PRAYERS AND REQUESTS. WITH THIS IN MIND, BE ALERT AND ALWAYS KEEP ON PRAYING FOR ALL THE SAINTS. EPHESIANS 6:14–18

Reflections

_____

_____

_____

_____

_____

_____

_____

_____

_____

_____

_____

_____

_____

_____

_____

_____

_____

_____

Pray

Dear Lord, help me to become intimately acquainted
with each piece of the armor you gave me so that
I might be victorious in the invisible war . . .

While it has become fashionable to credit the devil with every temptation we face, we must be ever mindful that spiritual warfare involves the world and the flesh as well.

Question: Have you ever been guilty of the devil-made-me-do-it theology? If so, what do you think are the dangers of this kind of thinking?

THE ONE WHO RECEIVED THE SEED THAT FELL AMONG THE THORNS IS THE MAN WHO HEARS THE WORD, BUT THE WORRIES OF THIS LIFE AND THE DECEITFULNESS OF WEALTH CHOKE IT, MAKING IT UNFRUITFUL. MATTHEW 13:22

Reflections

_____

_____

_____

_____

_____

_____

_____

_____

_____

_____

_____

_____

_____

_____

_____

_____

_____

_____

_____

_____

_____

Pray

Lord, help me neither to overestimate nor underestimate
the power and province of the devil . . .

When we pray "lead us not into temptation, but deliver us from the evil one," we are acknowledging that God is sovereign over all things, including the temptations of Satan. Augustine rightly referred to the evil one as "the ape of God."

Question: How has God helped you to resist the temptations of the world, the flesh, and the devil?

BE SELF-CONTROLLED AND ALERT. YOUR ENEMY THE DEVIL PROWLS AROUND LIKE A ROARING LION LOOKING FOR SOMEONE TO DEVOUR. RESIST HIM, STANDING FIRM IN THE FAITH. 1 PETER 5:8–9

Reflections

_____
_____
_____
_____
_____
_____
_____
_____
_____
_____
_____
_____
_____
_____
_____
_____
_____
_____

Pray

Lord, I thank you that while our enemy the devil prowls around like
a roaring lion looking for someone to devour, he is a lion on a leash
the length of which is determined by your sovereign wisdom . . .

Whenever we pray "lead us not into temptation, but deliver us from the evil one," we are reminded to look forward to the day when we will be completely set free from all temptations. The very fact that Jesus withstood the temptations in the wilderness and later in his ministry is our guarantee that one day soon the kingdom will be ours.

Question: What did the temptation of Jesus demonstrate?

NOTHING IMPURE WILL EVER ENTER IT, NOR WILL ANYONE WHO DOES WHAT IS SHAMEFUL OR DECEITFUL, BUT ONLY THOSE WHOSE NAMES ARE WRITTEN IN THE LAMB'S BOOK OF LIFE. REVELATION 21:27

Reflections

_____

_____

_____

_____

_____

_____

_____

_____

_____

_____

_____

_____

_____

_____

_____

_____

_____

_____

_____

Pray

Lord Jesus, thank you that one day soon
the tempter will be thrown into the lake of burning
sulfur and temptations will be no more . . .

chapter nine

Into the Deep

Deep is where we step out of the shallow tide pool of our hearts into the boundless ocean of God's power and presence. It is where we get beyond surface things and plunge into a deep relationship with our Creator.

Question: Why does Jesus want you to venture out of the shallow waters of prayer?

AS THE DEER PANTS FOR STREAMS OF WATER, SO MY SOUL PANTS FOR YOU, O GOD. PSALM 42:1

Reflections

_____

_____

_____

_____

_____

_____

_____

_____

_____

_____

_____

_____

_____

_____

_____

_____

_____

_____

Pray

Lord Jesus, I thank you that the prayer you taught
us to pray is an entryway into an ever-deepening
experience with my precious heavenly Father . . .

Going deep with God begins with a major paradigm shift in our perceptions about prayer. Rather than looking for techniques through which we can get God to answer our prayers, we must be ever mindful that prayer is an opportunity for developing intimacy with the very One who knit us together in our mothers' wombs.

Question: Are you guilty of wanting a relationship with God without the discipline of investing in quality time?

HOW PRECIOUS TO ME ARE YOUR THOUGHTS, O GOD! HOW VAST IS THE SUM OF THEM! WERE I TO COUNT THEM, THEY WOULD OUTNUMBER THE GRAINS OF SAND. WHEN I AWAKE, I AM STILL WITH YOU. PSALM 139:17–18

Reflections

_____

_____

_____

_____

_____

_____

_____

_____

_____

_____

_____

_____

_____

_____

_____

_____

_____

_____

Pray

Dear Lord, forgive me for a life that has manifested less of an
interest in my Master than in what is on the Master's table . . .

He has sent us sixty-six love letters etched in heavenly handwriting. And the more we meditate upon those words, the clearer his voice will resonate in the sounds of our silence.

Question: How do the words of Scripture help us hear God's voice?

_____

_____

_____

_____

_____

_____

_____

_____

_____

_____

THEN A GREAT AND POWERFUL WIND TORE THE MOUNTAINS APART AND SHATTERED THE ROCKS BEFORE THE LORD, BUT THE LORD WAS NOT IN THE WIND. AFTER THE WIND THERE WAS AN EARTHQUAKE, BUT THE LORD WAS NOT IN THE EARTHQUAKE. AFTER THE EARTHQUAKE CAME A FIRE, BUT THE LORD WAS NOT IN THE FIRE. AND AFTER THE FIRE CAME A GENTLE WHISPER.

1 KINGS 19:11B–12

Reflections

_____

_____

_____

_____

_____

_____

_____

_____

_____

_____

_____

_____

_____

_____

_____

_____

_____

_____

_____

_____

Pray

As Samuel said in 1 Samuel 3:10,
"Speak, Lord, for your servant is listening . . ."

We desperately need a place away from the invasive sounds of this world so that we can hear the sounds of another place and another voice.

Question: Do you have a secret place where you can drown out the static of the world and hear the voice of your heavenly Father?

YOU ARE MY HIDING PLACE; YOU WILL PROTECT ME FROM TROUBLE AND SURROUND ME WITH SONGS OF DELIVERANCE. PSALM 32:7

Reflections

Pray

Dear Lord, I treasure the privilege of being
alone with you in our secret place . . .

chapter ten

Embracing the Prayer of Jesus

The secret to prayer is secret prayer. Your public presence is a direct reflection of your private prayer life. If you spend time in the secret place, you will exude peace in the midst of life's storms.

Question: Are you a poster-child for Christianity or "busy-anity"? What can you do to make tangible changes to your frenzied lifestyle?

PEACE I LEAVE WITH YOU; MY PEACE I GIVE YOU. I DO NOT GIVE TO YOU AS THE WORLD GIVES. DO NOT LET YOUR HEARTS BE TROUBLED AND DO NOT BE AFRAID. JOHN 14:27

Reflections

_____

_____

_____

_____

_____

_____

_____

_____

_____

_____

_____

_____

_____

_____

_____

_____

_____

_____

Pray

Lord, help me to reflect your person and your presence . . .

Make prayer a priority. Wisdom is the application of knowledge.

Question: How can you best apply what you have learned from your study of the Lord's Prayer?

THEREFORE EVERYONE WHO HEARS THESE WORDS OF MINE AND PUTS THEM INTO PRACTICE IS LIKE A WISE MAN WHO BUILT HIS HOUSE ON THE ROCK.

MATTHEW 7:24

Reflections

Pray

Lord, help me to make my time with you
the highest priority of my day . . .

Prayer is a beautiful foretaste of something we will experience for all eternity. Paradise lost will soon be Paradise restored and a whole lot more. For we will experience something not even Adam and Eve experienced—face-to-face communication with the very One who taught us the prayer of Jesus.

Question: Write out the Lord's Prayer, meditating on each powerful thought.

NOW WE SEE BUT A POOR REFLECTION AS IN A MIRROR; THEN WE SHALL SEE FACE TO FACE. NOW I KNOW IN PART; THEN I SHALL KNOW FULLY, EVEN AS I AM FULLY KNOWN. 1 CORINTHIANS 13:12

Reflections

_____

_____

_____

_____

_____

_____

_____

_____

_____

_____

_____

_____

_____

_____

_____

_____

_____

_____

_____

_____

Pray

Dear Lord, I long to forever explore the glory
and grandeur of your grace and greatness . . .

Building Our Relationship

Our Father in heaven…I thank you that though you transcend time and space we can address you with intimacy. I am so grateful that through the sacrifice of your Son on the cross we may legitimately refer to you as "our Father." I come to you with a humble faith in your love and resources. I confess my unworthiness and thank you for your saving and sanctifying grace and for your goodness in supplying all my needs . . .

Hallowed be your name…I pray that today my life would radiate the unique reverence that your holiness demands; that your Word would be preached without corruption; that our churches be led by faithful pastors and preserved from false prophets; that I might be kept from language that profanes your name; that my thought life would be pure; and that I would cease from seeking honor for myself and seek instead that your name would be glorified . . .

Your kingdom come…I ask dear Lord that you would expand your rule over the territory of my heart. Please use the witness of my life, love, and lips for the extension of your kingdom. I so look forward to the day that the enemy shall totally and finally surrender and we will enter the golden city with divine assurance that nothing impure will ever enter it . . .

Your will be done on earth as it is in heaven…I thank you heavenly Father that this world is under your control, not mine; I submit my will to you confident that you have every detail of my life under control; you do not spare me from trial and tribulation but you use the fiery furnace to purge the impurities from my life . . .

Bringing Our Requests

Give us today our daily bread...I thank you for providing all things necessary for the sustenance of my body and life. I do not pray for my needs alone, but for the needs of my extended family as well. Please provide for those throughout the world who suffer daily from maladies ranging from droughts to deadly diseases. And help me to be ever mindful that I cannot rightly pray, "give," and not be a giver myself . . .

Forgive us our debts, as we also have forgiven our debtors...Our Father, if there is unforgiveness in my heart, please motivate me to work toward the process of genuine reconciliation and the willingness to forgive as I have been forgiven. If for even a moment I might wonder whether or not to forgive, please soften my heart and illumine the darkness of my mind . . .

And lead us not into temptation but deliver us from the evil one...Lord, even as I pray "deliver us," I am reminded to put on the armor that you provided so that I can take my stand against the devil's schemes. I pray that I might stand firm with the belt of truth buckled around my waist, with the breastplate of righteousness in place, and with my feet fitted with the readiness that comes from the gospel of peace. In addition to all this help me to take up the shield of faith so that I can extinguish all the flaming arrows of the evil one. May I take up the helmet of salvation and the sword of the Spirit, which is the word of God. And with this in mind, may I be alert and always keep on praying in the Spirit for all the saints.

For yours is the kingdom and the power and the glory forever. Amen